Animal Family

Dogs

Paul Mason

Raintree
Chicago, Illinois

Edited by Nancy Dickmann and Laura Knowles
Designed by Philippa Jenkins
Original illustrations © Clare Elsom
Illustrations by Clare Elsom
Picture research by Liz Alexander
Originated by Capstone Global Library, Ltd.
Printed and bound in China by CTPS

16 15 14 13 12
10 9 8 7 6 5 4 3 2 1

**Library of Congress Cataloging-in-Publication
Data**
Mason, Paul, 1967-
  Dogs / Paul Mason.—1st ed.
    p. cm.—(Animal family albums)
  Includes bibliographical references and index.
  ISBN 978-1-4109-4936-3 (hb)—ISBN 978-1-4109-
4941-7 (pb) 1. Dogs—Juvenile literature. 2. Dog
breeds—Juvenile literature. I. Title.

  SF426.5.M274 2013
  636.7'1—dc23   2012013028

Acknowledgments
We would like to thank the following for permission
to reproduce photographs: Alamy pp. 13 (© Charles
Mistral), 16 (© David Cole), 26 (© Graham Franks);
Getty Images p. 27 (Jupiterimages/Brand X Pictures);
Nature Picture Library pp. 6 (© Bruce Davidson),
23 (© Bartussek / ARCO), 24 (© Edwin Giesbers);
Shutterstock pp. 4 (© cynoclub), 5 (© Marcel
Jancovic), 7 (© Gina Smith), 8 (© Eric Isselée),
9 (© Sergey Lavrentev), 11 (© Dale A Stork), 12
(© Mars Evis), 14 (© Shutter Lover), 17 (© Jagodka),
18 (© cynoclub), 19 (© photocell), 20 (© Daniel
Gale), 21 (© K. Kolygo), 22 (© Chris Kruger);
SuperStock pp. 10 (© Juniors), 15 (© Corbis),
25 (© Juniors).

Design elements reproduced with permission of
Shutterstock/© urfin (pencil); Shutterstock/
© Julia Ivantsova (pencil); Shutterstock/
© Studio DMM Photography, Designs & Art
(photo corners); Shutterstock/© wanchai (Blue
leather background); Shutterstock/© Sweet Lana
(blue pattern background).

Cover photographs of dogs reproduced with
permission of Shutterstock/© Erik Lam (Bloodhound),
Shutterstock/© Jagodka (Pug puppy), Shutterstock/
© Fesus Robert (Hungarian Puli dog), Shutterstock/
© Eric Isselée (Jack Russell).

Every effort has been made to contact copyright
holders of material reproduced in this book. Any
omissions will be rectified in subsequent printings if
notice is given to the publisher.

All the Internet addresses (URLs) given in this book
were valid at the time of going to press. However, due
to the dynamic nature of the Internet, some addresses
may have changed, or sites may have changed or
ceased to exist since publication. While the author and
publisher regret any inconvenience this may cause
readers, no responsibility for any such changes can be
accepted by either the author or the publisher.

Contents

Some words are printed in bold, **like this**. You can find out what they mean by looking in the glossary.

Meet the Family!

No one is sure how humans and wolves first began to live together. Perhaps extra-bold wolves came up to a campfire in search of scraps. Or perhaps humans found some wolf cubs and took them in.

Tame wolves turned out to be very useful. They warned if danger threatened the camp. They went hunting, helping to **track** and kill **prey**.

No matter what their size or shape is, every dog you meet is **descended** from wolves.

My name is Bob. I will be introducing you to some of my family members. I am a Basset Hound. You can find out more about my **breed** on page 14.

Wolves and humans first began to work together more than 10,000 years ago.

Wolves became dogs

As time went by, the tamed wolves became less wolf-like. Some became smaller and were good at catching rats. Others became slim and fast and were good at chasing deer. The fiercest dogs were used for guard duty.

Today, some types of dog have become so specialized that they look similar to each other and different from other types of dog. These are known as breeds. Dogs that are a mix of different breeds are called **mongrels**.

Some of my cousins still live in the wild. They never bathe or even get a haircut! Even so, we pet dogs have a lot in common with them.

This pack of African hunting dogs is working together to track down its **prey**.

Food

Wild dogs and wolves eat meat. **Packs** of wolves **track** and kill large animals, such as moose. Smaller wild dogs eat rabbits, mice, and even birds. Like their wild cousins, pet dogs need a meat-based diet.

A pet dog's pack is made up of its human family.

Living in a Pack

In the wild, dogs and wolves live in packs. The members do everything together, including hunting and eating. On cold nights, they huddle together in their **den** to keep warm. Pet dogs also like to be in a pack and hate being left alone. Luckily, dogs are happy to be in a pack made up of a human family—as long as they have plenty of company, they don't mind!

FAMILY SECRET

People say you can figure out a dog's age in human years by multiplying its real age by seven. This is roughly true for big dogs, but multiply by five for smaller dogs.

Lap Dogs

Some dogs like nothing more than to curl up on a human's warm lap. Personally, I prefer to be outdoors!

Pugs first appeared hundreds of years ago, in China. They became especially popular in a cold place called Tibet. The local **monks** sat with a Pug on their lap and tucked their hands under the dog for warmth.

Pug

Pugs are friendly little dogs that enjoy playing games as well as cuddling. Pugs have thick **coats** and do not enjoy hot days. The folds of skin around their noses mean they wheeze a lot. Pugs also snore!

In French, papillon means "butterfly." The Papillon gets its name from the shape of its ears.

Papillon

It would not be a surprise if Papillons were a bit snobby. After all, it was France's most famous king, Louis the Fourteenth, who first made the **breed** popular. King Louis liked Papillons because they are such intelligent little dogs. Papillons enjoy being trained and playing games—several times a day, if possible.

FAMILY SECRET

When Papillons first appeared, not all of them had ears that stood up. The ones with floppy ears became known as *phalene*—French for "moth."

9

Some members of my family just love to work. These dogs are full of energy. Their idea of a fun day out is herding sheep in the rain!

Pulis are unusual—but once you have seen one, you never forget its crazy coat!

Puli

Most Pulis have their thick **coats** knotted into cords by their owners. These thick knots mean drying a wet Puli is a long, tricky job! The Puli's **ancestors** stopped sheep from running away by jumping on the sheep and forcing them to roll onto their backs. Pulis bark a lot and are very protective of their family. This means they make good guard dogs.

Border Collie

Don't get a Border Collie unless you like long walks! These dogs are designed to run around herding sheep all day. A Border Collie that has to stay indoors soon gets miserable. Border Collies love learning new things, and they are fast and **agile**. They enjoy obedience classes, dog obstacle courses, and games.

This Border Collie is halfway around an obstacle course—and he's really enjoying it!

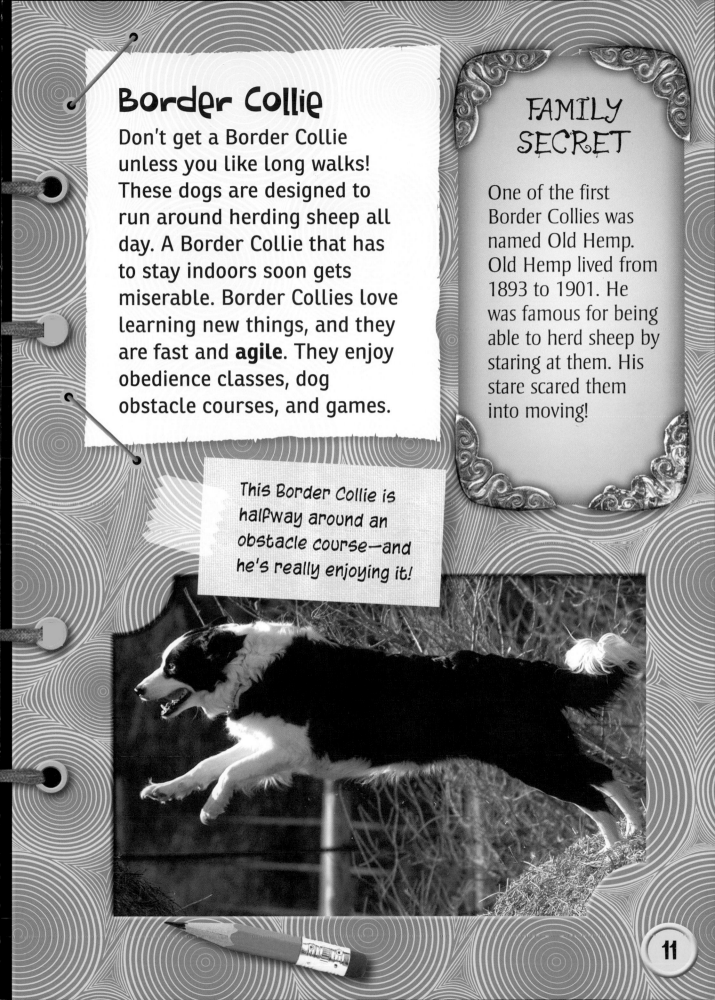

Water Dogs

I don't like swimming very much, but some of my cousins do. These two love charging into the water—even if it is really cold!

Labradors were bred to **retrieve** birds shot down over water.

Labrador Retriever

It is easy to see why Labradors are one of the most popular **breeds** of dog. They are friendly, playful, and easy to train. Labrador owners do need somewhere to dry off a wet dog, though. A Labrador's favorite game is running into water to fetch a ball or stick!

Portuguese Water Dog

As you might guess from their name, Portuguese Water Dogs love to swim! They originally worked on fishing boats. The dogs would fetch equipment that had been lost overboard or would carry things between boats. They could even herd fish into nets!

FAMILY SECRET

Portuguese Water Dogs are great at swimming, as you'd expect. What might surprise you is that they have webbed toes!

Portuguese Water Dogs became world famous when President Obama got one, named Bo, in 2009.

Scent Hounds

It's time to meet a couple of the world's best sniffers! That is my own **breed**, the Basset Hound, and my good friend, the Bloodhound.

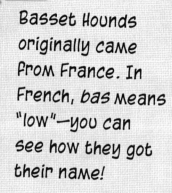

Basset Hounds originally came from France. In French, *bas* means "low"—you can see how they got their name!

Basset Hound

If you enjoy running, you should not get a Basset Hound—they cannot move very fast! Bassets are friendly, good-natured dogs. They can be very stubborn and hard to train, though. The thing Basset Hounds like most is sniffing their way along, nose to the ground. Once a Basset Hound gets a **scent**, it will walk long distances trying to find the end of the trail.

Bloodhound

Bloodhounds are some of the friendliest dogs around. The biggest problem with Bloodhounds is that they drool a lot! Bloodhounds are famous for their amazing sense of smell. It is several million times better than a human's. Bloodhounds have used their noses to **track** down escaped prisoners and people lost in the wilderness.

FAMILY SECRET

Bloodhounds can identify people by their smell. In the past, some courts of law accepted this identification as proof.

Bloodhounds can follow a scent left days before. One famous Bloodhound, named Nick Carter, followed a scent that was 10 days old.

Hunting Dogs

Like me, these next two **breeds** love to take part in a hunt. Unlike me, though, they are also fast moving and full of energy!

Springer Spaniels get their name from their ability to scare out—or "spring"—birds for hunters to shoot.

English Springer Spaniel

Springer Spaniels were bred to run around all day. They would flush out **game** for hunters or bring it back after it had been shot. This means they need lots of exercise. If you like long walks and throwing a ball to be brought back again and again, a Springer would be an ideal pet!

Pharaoh Hound

Pharaoh Hounds were once used for rabbit hunting. Hunters would send a ferret with a bell around its neck down the rabbit hole. The rabbit would run out—only to be grabbed by the waiting dog. Today, Pharaoh Hounds are usually kept as pets. They are good-natured and friendly, but they love to hunt. Never own a Pharaoh Hound alongside pet gerbils, hamsters...or rabbits!

FAMILY SECRET

When a Pharaoh Hound is excited, blood rushes to the dog's head, turning its nose and ears a glowing reddish color!

Pharaoh Hounds are thought to have come from ancient Egypt.

Rat Catchers

Now it is time to meet some tough relatives. These two were bred for catching rats. They never back down from a fight!

Many Jack Russell Terriers are **descended** from a dog named Trump, who was owned by a man named Jack Russell in the 1800s.

Jack Russell Terrier

You need a good fence if you have a Jack Russell. Otherwise, it will escape and go exploring! The Jack Russell is one of the most intelligent dogs around. Some even figure out how to *climb* fences! Jack Russells are usually pleased to meet strangers and they play happily with children.

Fox Terrier

Fox Terriers have appeared in many movies. For example, Tintin's dog, Snowy, is a Fox Terrier. Fox Terriers are fierce hunters of rats. If a Fox Terrier spots a rat, it grabs it by the back of the neck. Then it shakes the rat violently from side to side, which breaks the rat's neck. Fox Terriers love their owners, but they can be a bit snobby toward other people or dogs.

FAMILY SECRET

There are two types of Fox Terrier: **wire-haired** and **smooth**. The photo below shows a dog with a wire-haired **coat**.

Fox Terriers were bred mainly for hunting rats.

Dogs to the Rescue!

> Some of my relatives just love the cold! It gives them a chance to get outside and rescue a human in distress.

Newfoundlands are tough, strong dogs. Their webbed feet help them swim well.

Newfoundland

Newfoundlands are amazingly strong. They were originally used on land and in the water. They could help gather in fishing nets and even rescue drowning people. Today, some Newfoundlands are trained as lifeguards and spend their time rescuing swimmers in trouble. Newfoundlands are sweet-natured, friendly dogs, and many are kept as pets. Watch out, though—their big, saggy mouths do mean that they drool a lot and are messy eaters!

Saint Bernard

With their thick **coats** and digging skills, Saint Bernards were bred for rescuing travelers caught in sudden snowstorms. They have an excellent sense of smell and can even sniff out people buried by **avalanches**. The dogs lick people's faces to wake them. Then they lie beside them to provide warmth until help arrives.

FAMILY SECRET

One Saint Bernard, named Barry, is said to have saved the lives of at least 40 people. Barry lived in Switzerland between 1800 and 1814.

Saint Bernards have been rescuing humans in distress for hundreds of years.

The Wild Bunch

Some of my cousins still live in the wild. Sadly, they don't have very good manners—they would probably bite you if you tried to pet them.

The African hunting dog is sometimes called the "painted wolf."

African hunting dogs

African hunting dogs live in the grasslands and woodlands of Africa. Their big teeth and extremely powerful jaws easily crunch through bone. African hunting dogs hunt in **packs**. They work as a team, communicating with barks and yips. The dogs are almost three times more successful at hunting than lions. They mainly hunt antelope and young wildebeest.

This family of Australian dingoes is well-fed and happy—and like all cubs, these dingoes are very playful.

Dingoes

Dingoes come from Australia. They are large, wolf-like dogs that live in packs. Dingoes do not always hunt together, and they are often seen alone. Their main **prey** includes kangaroos, **wallabies**, cows, rabbits, and rats. But dingoes will eat almost anything, from human garbage to fish or insects!

FAMILY SECRET

Through the years, a few dingoes gave up the wild to live with humans. **Aboriginal Australians** have kept dingoes as pets for thousands of years. Today, some other Australians do the same.

Wolf Pack!

Last of all, it is time to meet the original head of the family—the gray wolf.

These young wolves are play-fighting—practicing for when they are fully grown.

Pack territory

Wolves live in **packs**. Each wolf pack has a **territory**, which it defends against other packs. Some wolf packs have giant territories. One pack in Alaska had a territory that was 2,420 square miles (6,270 square kilometers). That is more than 10 times the size of the city of Chicago!

Wolves are amazingly strong for their size. A single wolf can turn over the frozen body of a horse or moose.

FAMILY SECRET

Wolves have lots of ways of communicating. These include making faces, body positions, marking objects with their smell, and all sorts of howls and growls.

Food and hunting

A wolf pack spends all its time moving around its territory, looking for **prey**. The wolves prefer to kill and eat large animals such as moose or deer. Wolves will eat almost anything, though, including salmon, birds, and humans' garbage. Although wolves are not usually dangerous to humans, they have been known to kill and eat people.

New Dogs

Puppies are cute and cuddly, but they are hard work! Their owners have to do everything their mother would do in the wild. A puppy has to be fed several times a day. It must be kept warm and played with (that part is easy!). And you have to clean up its pee and poop!

Most puppies arrive at their new home when they are just 8 to 10 weeks old.

Older dogs and mongrels

Adopting an older dog may be easier than getting a puppy. It will have learned not to go to the bathroom indoors! Also, giving a home to an older dog means it will not have to live in a cage at an animal shelter anymore.

Many people prefer **mongrels** to dogs from a particular **breed**. Mongrels usually have fewer health problems and live longer.

This family has decided to give a home to a dog that has been abandoned.

Everyone loves puppies, but they can be naughty! If you are like me and prefer a quiet life, a grown-up dog may make a better pet.

What Type of Dog Are You?

You are not a dog, of course—you're a human. But dog and human personalities can seem very similar. What kind of dog would your personality make you?

1. On a snowy day, what would be your idea of fun?

a) Stay indoors beside a warm fire and watch TV.

b) Go outside and start diving into snow banks, trying to discover what's hidden under the surface. There could be rats!

c) Play outside all day. And all night. And all the next day.

2. If someone suggests a team game, do you?

a) Agree to watch—as long as there is somewhere comfortable to sit, that is!

b) Insist that it is a game of chase—ideally, chasing rats!

c) Call the rink to reserve ice time to play ice hockey.

3. Where do you prefer to sleep?

a) On a soft bed, with soft sheets and a hot water bottle, beside a radiator.

b) In a barn on straw—but you like to stay half awake in case any rats appear.

c) An igloo.

4. What's your favorite thing to eat?

a) Tasty snacks all through the day (they must be fed to you by hand!).

b) Rats! No, just kidding, you don't actually eat rats. You'll eat whatever's put in front of you.

c) A warming meat stew.

5. Where would you prefer to live?

a) It has to be a palace, but I don't actually mind which country the palace is in.

b) New York—there are many rats there.

c) Iceland.

Answers

Mostly a: You like to be comfortable, warm, and well cared for—you are definitely a lap dog, such as a Pug.

Mostly b: With your lively personality and interest in rats, you would have to be a terrier, such as a Jack Russell.

Mostly c: No one who likes the cold as much as you could be anything but a rescue dog, perhaps a Saint Bernard.

Glossary

Aboriginal Australian person whose distant relatives were the first humans to live in Australia

agile able to move around quickly and easily

ancestor relative that lived long ago

avalanche slide of snow, rock, and ice down a mountainside

breed particular type of one kind of animal. For example, a Fox Terrier is a particular breed of dog. All the members of a breed are a similar size and shape and they look alike.

coat dog's hair, which covers its skin and keeps it warm

den place where a dog or pack of dogs sleeps and rests

descended related to an ancestor

game wild animals or birds that are hunted for food or sport

mongrel dog that is a mix of different breeds

monk person who spends his life living as part of a religious group or community

pack group of dogs or wolves, usually all related to each other

prey animal that is hunted and eaten by another animal

retrieve bring something back. Retriever dogs were traditionally trained to bring back birds that had been shot down by hunters.

scent smell, or trail of smell, left behind

smooth with short hairs that lie flat against the dog's skin

territory area of land that an animal sees as its own space

track follow using scent, sound, and other signs

wallaby small, kangaroo-like animal

wire-haired with longer hairs that are thick and wiry, with a rough appearance

Find Out More

Books

Barnes, Julia. *Pet Dogs* (Pet Pals). Milwaukee: Gareth Stevens, 2007.

Ganeri, Anita. *Dogs* (A Pet's Life). Chicago: Heinemann Library, 2009.

Lewis, J. Patrick. *First Dog*. Chelsea, Mich.: Sleeping Bear, 2009.

Paley, Rebecca. *Dogs 101*. New York: Scholastic, 2010.

Web sites

Facthound offers a safe, fun way to find web sites related to this book. All the sites on Facthound have been researched by our staff.

Here's all you do:
Visit www.facthound.com
Type in this code: 9781410949363

Index